Financial Convergence

A Powerful Model for Creating More Income with Less Risk

DAVE BJORKLUND

FINANCIAL CONVERGENCE

A Powerful Model for Creating More
Income with Less Risk

2017 David A. Bjorklund

Box 715
Monument, CO 80132-0715

Printed in the United States of America
First Printing in 2017

Cover Design by Corrin Brewer

Table of Contents

Disclaimer

Much effort has been taken to provide accurate and current information regarding the material covered in this book. However, Dave Bjorklund, Compass Associates, Inc. DBA The Compass Group, and none of its employees or affiliates assume responsibility for any errors or omissions or the results that individual readers create from using this material.

The title, *Financial Convergence. A Powerful Strategy for Creating More Income-Less Risk,* is just that: a title. It does not guarantee that you will accomplish what is implied in the title. In fact, there is likely no financial book that can guarantee the results upon which it is focused.

There may be local, state, or federal regulations which impact the application of ideas and strategies outlined in this book. The contents of this book are intended for informational purposes only. Thus, there is no guarantee of comprehensiveness nor accuracy regarding the results that are achieved from using the information in this book. Your use of the ideas, strategies, and financial vehicles described in this book are to be done at your own risk.

In no way will Dave Bjorklund, Compass Associates, Inc. DBA The Compass Group, nor any of its heirs, successors, nor assigns, or any of its employees or affiliates be liable to you or anyone else to whom you give this book to read, for the decisions you make or do not make based on the information in this book.

Neither Dave Bjorklund, Compass Associates, Inc. DBA The Compass Group, nor any of its employees or affiliates are engaged in providing legal, accounting, tax, or other professional services. If these types of services are desired and required, then the services of professionals in these areas should be sought.

The information in this book is believed to be accurate at the time of publication. This information could become outdated because of new or revised laws, financial conditions, or other circumstances. All of the charts and projections are based on assumptions and rates no later in time than December, 2016. The rates and assumptions in this book are not guaranteed and are subject to change. The illustrations and projections in this book will use product information and projections from life insurance carriers. These numbers are subject to change based on the future performance of the life insurance products referenced. There can be other factors that would alter the numbers in the charts and projections, including, but not limited to, the individual's situation, location, state laws, health, and tax bracket.

The client examples used in this book are for illustration purposes only and some of the details have been changed to protect client information. The names have been changed as well.

As previously stated, all contents of this book are to be used for informational purposes only. Any negative comments or observations against individuals, companies, or organizations are unintentional.

You, the reader, are solely responsible for the use of the information in this book and hold Dave Bjorklund, Compass Associates, Inc. DBA The Compass Group, its employees and affiliates harmless in any event or claim.

Introduction

"Of all history, the most important to a man is his own"

Jim Rohn

MY PERSONAL HISTORY LESSON

Let's start with a bold statement:

Yes, it is possible to create a financial strategy to both maximize retirement income and minimize risk.

**Do you want to sleep well at night with no concerns about
when the next stock market crash is coming?
Do you want to enjoy your retirement years without
having to check the Dow every morning?
Are you tired of the Wall Street propaganda,
"Don't worry about
the market downturns, it will come back,
just be patient," as you
watch your nest egg evaporate?**

I have spent the past 13,000 days of my life providing financial ideas and strategies to business owners, professionals and working families.

It has been said that we should learn something new every day. That may be a stretch. However, if I have learned just one important and transferrable financial principle each year, that would arm me today with 35 powerful strategies for the benefit of my clients . . . and you, my reader.

More Income – Less Risk

This book reflects much of what I have learned about money over these 35 years, and specifically, how you can **create more retirement income with less risk.** Stop and think about that statement. Is that not what most everyone is looking for in their retirement planning? Sure beats less income and more risk, which is the case for many.

Financial Convergence

The strategies presented here are based on a concept that I call **Financial Convergence.** Throughout the book, I will provide definitions, examples, charts, diagrams and action steps on how you can create financial convergence in your retirement planning.

In Chapter 1, I will explain **the convergence concept**. Then throughout the rest of the book, I will demonstrate the step-by-step process on how to:

- Use financial convergence to make the right financial decisions.
- Identify the financial strategies that are right for you.
- Build your **Financial Convergence Roadmap.**
- Select the best financial vehicles to accomplish YOUR financial goals.

Once you capture the essence of financial convergence and follow its principles, you will be empowered with newfound clarity and simplicity in your financial decision-making.

My client work today is all about convergence. Rather than telling my clients what to do, I simply come alongside and teach them how to create their own financial convergence.

How about no second-guessing your financial decisions anymore? Sound good? I will show you how.

Financial Coaching Manual

I have intentionally designed this book to be a hands-on resource to which you can refer as often as necessary. In addition, by using the convergence resources found in this book, you will create a personalized retirement planning reference manual to use for the rest of your life.

Sleep well

Almost everyone I encounter these days has some angst about the stock market and how it may affect their personal financial future. Even those who seem outwardly comfortable leaving 100 percent of their retirement assets at the whim of the Wall Street Gurus will, when honest, admit their concerns. With the strategies outlined here, there will be no more waking up at 2:00 a.m. and fretting over whether or not you made the right financial decisions. Hard to put a price tag on peace of mind.

As you adapt these strategies to your personal financial circumstances, angst will fade away and confidence will emerge.

The book is divided into three sections:

- **Part 1. Roadmaps.** I teach you how to create your own Financial Convergence Roadmap.
- **Part 2. Resources.** I provide information on financial strategies designed to help you create more income with less risk.
- **Part 3. Results.** I demonstrate how the application of our financial convergence principles in retirement planning really works.

Here's the simple, but powerful, success formula outlined in this book:

ROADMAPS + RESOURCES = RESULTS

PART 1

ROADMAPS

1

The Power in Convergence

"In the end, it's not the years in your life that counts, it's the life in your years."

Abraham Lincoln

MY INTRODUCTION TO CONVERGENCE

At the time, the word convergence was not in my vocabulary. But even then, back in junior high school, my internal compass was tugging at me to create a life built around my passions and unique ability. I am a teacher-coach at heart. I love helping talented and motivated people become the best that they can be.

And so, a few years ago, when I used the Assessment Tool in Tom Rath's best-selling book, *Strength's Finder*, it was not surprising that what emerged as #1 for me was what Rath calls Maximizer[1]. He summarizes Maximizer this way: "Strengths, whether yours or someone else's fascinate you. Having found a strength, you feel compelled to nurture it, refine it, and stretch it toward excellence."

Following college, my first career as a high school math teacher and basketball coach provided a great environment to do just that. Without realizing it at the time, the decisions I was making around my passions were creating a life of convergence.

Eight years later, my teaching and coaching moved from the classroom and basketball court to kitchen tables and conference rooms. Convergence continued for me as I began to teach and coach my clients on how to design a financial plan which matched their values and goals. Long before I had coined the phrase, I was helping talented and motivated people create more freedom and simplicity in their lives through financial convergence. My maximizer passion continued to drive me.

So, when I first stumbled across the concept of convergence some 20 years later, it put helpful context around what I was already doing. In his book, *The Making of a Leader*, Dr. Robert Clinton outlined the convergence process in the framework of helping leaders maximize their full potential. With my Maximizer strength, this was intriguing to me. Here's my summary of what Clinton said about convergence:

Convergence occurs when the leader's skills, past experiences, passions, knowledge, time, unique abilities, financial resources, and relationships all work in harmony [converge] to fulfill the leader's vision and life purpose.[2]

The dictionary defines convergence as:

to meet in a point or line or to tend to a common result.

BROAD APPLICATIONS

Since that more formal introduction to convergence from Dr. Clinton's book, I was motivated to explore the broader scope of its applications, one of which is the focus of this book – **how to use financial convergence to create more income with less risk.** Our proprietary **Financial Convergence Roadmap** is one of the tools which emerged from my many years of researching and testing convergence.

CONVERGENCE MINDSET

Before we delve into Financial Convergence in Chapter 2, however, it is important to gain a solid grasp of the convergence principles and the power created from its application in your life. Developing a **convergence mindset** will impact not only your finances, but how you both achieve goals and deal with life's challenges.

CONVERGENCE IN NATURE

The Chippewa Indians named it, "The Big River." As a child, my brothers and I navigated the rocks at its Lake Itasca headwaters just 100 miles north of the central Minnesota farm where I was born and raised. From that quiet, unassuming beginning, the Mississippi River winds its way 2,450 miles to the Gulf of Mexico. Along the way, 40 tributaries, including the Missouri and Arkansas, converge into The Big River capturing millions of gallons of surging water from one-third of the land surface of the United States.

The Mississippi paints a vivid picture of convergence in nature. By itself, the Mississippi would be nothing more than a meandering creek in northern Minnesota. But with its many converging tributaries, the Mississippi swells into an ever-increasing force, surging with power, and cutting its own path to the Gulf of Mexico.

And just as convergent river water creates a force of strength and energy in nature, so does convergence in your life and mine.

GOAL

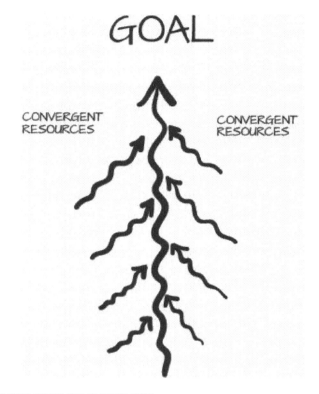

CONVERGENT
RESOURCES

CONVERGENT
RESOURCES

CONVERGENCE DEFINED:

**Convergence occurs when the resources
(tributaries)
necessary to accomplish your vision or goal
(The Big River)
work in harmony (converge)
enabling you to achieve your desired results in the
most
effective manner possible.**

EXAMPLES OF CONVERGENT LIVES

Throughout history, we find examples of men and women who lived lives of convergence and impacted their world for much good.

From **Alexande**r the Great to Napoleon **Bonaparte**;

from Abraham **Lincoln** to Winston **Churchill**;

from George Washington **Carver** to Henry **Ford**;

from Mother **Theresa** to Martin Luther **King**.

The list goes on and on.

Unfortunately, there are also examples of men and women whose life resources converged around an evil goal – people like Leopold II, Tojo, Hitler, Stalin, Zedong, and many others.

THE COMMON CHARACTERISTICS

You will find two common characteristics for all who experience the power of convergence in their lives:

- First, each had a **Big River:** a powerful vision, dream, purpose or goal which consumed their lives.

  For Alexander the Great, it was spreading the Greek culture
  around the world.
  For Napoleon Bonaparte, it was developing his code of legal reforms.
  For Abraham Lincoln, it was preserving the Union and eliminating slavery.
  For Winston Churchill, it was defeating Hitler and
  saving the world from widespread tyranny.
  For George Washington Carver, it was improving lives by finding
  hundreds of uses for the peanut.
  For Henry Ford, it was producing an affordable car for the masses.
  For Mother Theresa, it was lifting up the poor in India.
  For Martin Luther King, it was creating racial equality.

- Second, they each maximized their **life resources** – their thinking, imagination, energy, unique abilities, past experiences, financial resources, time, relationships and habits. These resources all converged into their Big River creating ever-increasing momentum and breakthroughs to accomplish their vision and purpose.

Bill Gaither – Modern Day Example of a Convergent Life

Bill Gaither was born on March 28, 1936. Though raised on the family farm near Anderson, Indiana, his interest was not in taking over the family farm. In 1959, he began teaching high school English. Yet it was his passion for music which dominated his thinking, imagination, time, and energy.

 In 1962, Bill married Gloria Sickel who shared both his talent and love for music. For the next five years, Bill and Gloria juggled two careers. The first career, teaching, paid the bills. But it was the second career, singing and songwriting, which captured their hearts.

"He Touched Me," recorded in 1964, was their breakthrough song. Over the next decade, they composed hundreds of songs, many of which are among the all-time greats in gospel music and are still sung today throughout the world.

But his life of convergence around music did not stop there. Actually, it was just beginning:

- The Gaither Vocal Band was formed in 1981 and is still performing today. In fact, my wife and I recently attended one of their inspiring concerts. Over the years, many talented artists have taken their turn in the vocal band and have been greatly enriched by both Bill's musical skills and his passion for mentoring.
- On February 19, 1991, his vision for showcasing top Southern Gospel talent from across the United States became a reality when the Gaither Homecoming Gatherings were born. Today, thousands of people flock to these unique and uplifting concerts and tens of thousands more bring its music into

their homes through the Gaither Video Collections.

And so, for 55 years and counting, Bill's passion for composing and performing gospel music, as well as showcasing both new and seasoned talent, has dominated his life. Now, at age 80, he continues to pursue his passion which is spotlighted when you watch the Gaither performances and see the sheer delight on Bill's face.

Tracing his life roadmap, it is powerfully evident how Bill's dreams, passions, unique abilities, time, energy, relationships and financial resources all converge into his "Big River."

As a result of pursuing his music dreams and modeling a life of convergence, the lives of hundreds of thousands of people have been enriched. And because of his generous heart focused on encouragement and mentoring, the careers of talented-but-little-known artists have been greatly enhanced, exponentially expanding the reach of their music.

THE CONVERGENT LIFE OF
BILL GAITHER

GOSPEL MUSIC
AMBASSADOR TO THE
WORLD

TIME

ENERGY

PASSIONS

UNIQUE
ABILITIES

VISION

RELATIONSHIPS

FINANCIAL
RESOURCES

MENTORING

SHOWCASING
TALENT

CONVERGENCE WITH YOUR DREAM:

What's your dream, vision, or big purpose in life?
Maybe it is clearly defined and you are on the fast
track to achieving it. Good for you. But perhaps it

has laid dormant for many years as life happens and time gets stretched. Maybe you have tried to pursue your dream in the past but hit roadblocks and became discouraged.

You were created in a unique way and for a unique purpose. You can discover your purpose by

- designing a Life Convergence Roadmap for the dreams and passions that lie within you, then
- deciding to take some bold, new steps toward making these dreams a reality.

It all starts with your dream, vision, purpose, your BHAG (Big, hairy, audacious goal as Jim Collins calls it in his book, *Built to Last*[3]). Your goal does not need to be of the magnitude of a Lincoln, Carver or Bonaparte — or it might be greater than theirs.

Your passion may be helping disadvantaged children in your neighborhood, starting a business and creating new jobs, mentoring young mothers, providing resources for the local food shelter, micro-finance projects in Uganda, encouraging wounded soldiers, promoting positive change through political efforts, improving your schools, or a host of other life-changing endeavors.

What turns your crank?

Where do your passions lie?

What are your unique abilities (we all have them)?

What past experiences have helped shape you?

What would truly energize you (besides dark-roast coffee) when you wake up in the morning?

Some of the resources (tributaries) available to help you accomplish your purpose, dream or goal would include your

creative ideas

habits developed

available time

knowledge base

people skills

communication skills

unique abilities

key decisions

past successes

lessons from past failures

financial resources

family members

personal mentors

key relationships

lives of leaders

and your deep passion and sense of calling

GETTING STARTED

Create your Life Convergence Roadmap

- Write down your goal (Big River) in as much detail as possible.
- List all available resources (tributaries) which will aid in the achievement of your goal.
- Determine specific strategies for each of these resources (you may find it helpful to create a convergence diagram around each resource).

- Use your Convergence Roadmap to encourage and guide you as you pursue your dream.

THE COMPOUND EFFECT

If the Mississippi River received water from one tributary, it would gain *some* strength. With two tributaries, the effect is more than double. And as each new tributary joins the "team," the power grows exponentially.

The same is true as you build convergent tributaries into your "Big River." The more tributaries (resources) you identify and direct toward your goal, the faster the "water" flows and the greater the chances of not only achieving your goal but surpassing it.

THE CONVERGENCE HABIT

Our behavior is guided by the habits we have built, good and bad. What makes a habit good is that it supports our goals, bad habits defeat our goals.

We have all acquired habits which greatly impact how we live our lives, some intentionally developed and some unintentional. Successful people are intentional about building success habits, and they have learned to align these habits with their goals.

A **convergence mindset** is a powerful habit. When developed, your approach to achieving a goal will be dramatically enhanced. My experience has been that it takes 90 days for a new habit to be firmly entrenched.

You will know when you have the habit of a convergence mindset firmly established in your life:

- You decide on a new goal or project and your mind immediately latches on to the convergence picture of the Mississippi and its tributaries.
- You then create a **Convergence Diagram** (the converging arrows pointed north) where you identify the key resources, which when "flowing together" will maximize the achievement of your goal.

DIVERGENCE

The opposite of convergence is **divergence**. When
river waters diverge, they lose their power and
begin to meander and seek the path of least
resistance. For many miles, the Mississippi River
meanders until enough tributaries flow into it to
create a force of water strong enough to cut its
own path and to remove the many obstacles
encountered. Without the fresh water from its
tributaries, the Mississippi would remain an
unknown and insignificant creek.

**Divergence (meandering)
occurs when you have not clearly identified
your goal, vision, dream
AND/OR
when your resources needed for achieving
that goal have not been identified or properly
aligned**

CONVERGENCE AT THE CORE:

- Identify your Big River
- Study those whose lives demonstrate convergence
- Develop the convergence habit
- Create a Personal Convergence Roadmap around a big goal
- Avoid divergence and meandering

WHAT'S NEXT?

In Chapter 2, we will begin exploring how to create **Financial Convergence.**

PART 1: ROADMAPS

2

Mastering
Financial
Convergence

"Before you speak, listen. Before you
write, think. Before you spend, earn.
Before you invest, investigate. Before you
criticize, wait. Before you pray, forgive.
Before you quit, try. Before you retire,
save. Before you die, give."

William A. Ward

Roger and Marcia are now retired. During their
working years, they carried on the frugal financial
values they had learned from both sets of parents
who had experienced the Great Depression. When

they reached retirement, Roger and Marcia had accumulated an impressive portfolio of retirement assets, especially considering their modest incomes.

In one of our **financial convergence discussions**, they said, "Now what? What financial strategies do we use during the retirement phase of our lives?" My response to their question was the same as it is with all my clients. **"What are your financial values and goals? Once those are clear, we can design a financial game plan that will create the financial convergence that you desire."**

And so, for the next hour, I helped them identify their key financial values and goals for their retirement years. Here's a summary of what they shared with me:

- We want guaranteed lifetime income.
- We do not want to worry about the next stock market crash.
- Safety of principal is very important to us.
- Keep things simple.
- We need liquidity for emergencies and opportunities.

- We are okay with annual returns of 5 percent to 7 percent with no risk of losses.
- We want to minimize income taxation wherever possible.
- We want to eliminate estate taxes.
- Maximizing the inheritances to our heirs is important to us.

It is impossible to create financial convergence without establishing clarity around your financial values and goals. Fortunately for Roger and Marcia, their values and goals were clear. This is not always the case, however.

I met recently with another couple, Steve and Linda who had given little thought to their financial future, even though they wanted to retire in a few years.

At our initial convergence discussion, they struggled to answer my values questions. Like many I encounter, they were simply hoping everything would work out. As I took the time to ask them clarifying questions, they became energized. The lights came on. By setting a simple framework for identifying their values and goals, they were motivated to be more thoughtful regarding their financial future. We have begun the process of creating their **Financial Convergence Roadmap**.

FINANCIAL CONVERGENCE DEFINED:

**Financial Convergence occurs when your financial strategies and financial vehicles (tributaries)
work in harmony (converge)
with your financial values and goals (Your Big River)
enabling you to achieve your desired results
in the most effective and efficient manner
possible.**

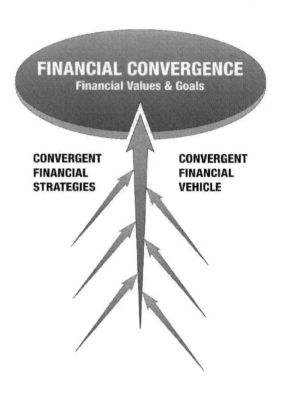

YOUR FINANCIAL CONVERGENCE JOURNEY:

A safe and enjoyable financial journey requires thoughtful planning and clear decision-making. Can you answer "yes" to the following?

- **Have you clearly defined your financial values and goals?**
- **Is this the grid through which you make financial decisions?**
- **Do your financial strategies line up with your financial values?**
- **Have you learned from financial mistake of the past?**

Lacking a clear process for financial decision-making often produces
an addiction to **hopeium,** which Wordnik defines as "an irrational or unwarranted optimism."

- **You hope the financial decisions you are making
will get you where you want to go.**
- **You hope the financial markets don't crash again.**
- **You hope that your adviser knows what he/she is doing.**

- **You hope that you can maintain your standard of living in retirement.**
- **You hope that taxes don't double.**

In addition, all the divergent noise from television commercials, newspaper ads, direct mail flyers, Wall Street "experts," well-meaning friends, seminar speakers (at least you get a free meal), E-mail marketers, and more, can create even greater confusion and frustration. Without a defined process, divergent decisions and second guessing will often rule the day.

There is a better way. Our **Financial Convergence Roadmap** is designed to help you:

- Simplify and clarify your financial decision-making.
- Create enhanced personal confidence and predictable results.
- Align your financial decisions with your values and goals.
- Achieve your financial goals effectively and efficiently.
- Sleep well at night.

Throughout the book, I will provide resources and strategies for designing your **Financial Convergence Roadmap**. Once created, it will become a most valuable resource throughout your financial journey.

CONVERGENCE ADVISERS

One of the challenges people face is finding an advisor with a convergence mindset. Is that true for you?

**How many of your financial advisers have helped you design a
Financial Convergence Roadmap?**

Have they had discussions with you around your financial values?

Have they provided guidance in clarifying your financial goals?

**How many have outlined the financial strategies and financial vehicles
which best converge with your goals and values?**

If not, why not?

SIX STEPS TO FINANCIAL CONVERGENCE

Step 1: IDENTIFY YOUR KEY FINANCIAL VALUES. Your financial values reflect what is most important to you regarding money and financial assets. Have you thought about your financial values? Be sure they are truly yours and not borrowed from someone else. Clarity around your financial values is where you must begin your financial convergence journey.

Step 2: WRITE DOWN YOUR KEY FINANCIAL GOALS. With your financial values identified, you next look at your financial goals. What are your key financial goals? When do you want to retire? What is your minimum retirement income? What is your desired retirement lifestyle? What are your financial legacy goals? Write them down for ongoing reference and review.

Step 3: DETERMINE THE FINANCIAL STRATEGIES WHICH BEST CONVERGE WITH YOUR VALUES AND GOALS. It is impossible to determine the right financial strategies if you have not first clarified your values and goals. However, once they are identified, you can now ask this simple question for each: "Does this financial strategy converge with my values and goals?"

Step 4: SELECT THE FINANCIAL VEHICLES WHICH BEST CONVERGE WITH YOUR VALUES,

GOALS AND STRATEGIES. In Chapter three, you will find an inventory of many of the financial vehicles available today. Clarity around your values, goals and strategies will greatly simplify the selection of your convergent financial vehicles.

Step 5: IMPLEMENT YOUR PLAN. This may involve repositioning some of your existing assets to create financial convergence. Depending on your specific assets, you may implement your full convergence plan immediately or do it in phases. For example, if you have an active 401(k) plan, and no in-service transfers are available, you will need to stay with the investment options provided in your plan until your age (59 ½) allows you to reposition to an IRA where you have much more flexibility.

Step 6: REVIEW AND REVISE. Because your financial life is dynamic, I recommend an annual review of your Financial Convergence Roadmap. As your circumstances change, make the appropriate course corrections.

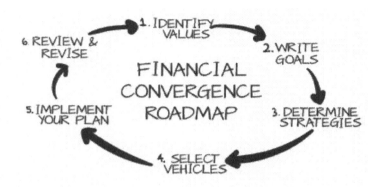

FINANCIAL DIVERGENCE AND MEANDERING

**Financial Divergence (meandering),
occurs when you have not clearly identified
your key financial values and goals
OR
when the financial strategies and vehicles that
you employ
do not align (converge) with your values and
goals.**

FINANCIAL
MEANDERING

CONVERGENCE AT THE CORE:

- Financial convergence begins with clarifying your financial values and goals.
- Find an adviser with a convergence mindset.
- Beware of financial divergence and addiction to hopeium.
- The financial convergence process will produce clarity, simplicity, confidence, and peace of mind.

WHAT'S NEXT?

In Chapter 3, we will begin the process of showing you how to create your own **Financial Convergence Roadmap**.

3

Your Financial Convergence Roadmap

"Being slow and steady means that you're willing to exchange the opportunity of making a killing for the assurance of never getting killed."

Carl Richards

In 1803, President Thomas Jefferson commissioned his personal secretary, Army Captain Meriwether Lewis to lead a three-year expedition into a vast unknown territory. Recently purchased from France for 15 million dollars (the real estate deal of the century) and known as the Louisiana Purchase, the 529 million acres stretched from the Mississippi

River to the west coast and virtually doubled the size of the United States overnight.

Lewis' task was to map out the land, find its best waterways, and confirm U. S. sovereignty to the region. He chose his good friend, Second Lieutenant William Clark, to join him in leading the Corps of Discovery Expedition. Departing from St. Louis in early May of 1804, the team of 33 began their dangerous 29-month journey to the west coast and back. When they reported their findings to Jefferson in September 1806, Clark produced a series of maps showing remarkable detail. These maps proved invaluable to the many who journeyed west for years to come.

YOUR FINANCIAL CONVERGENCE ROADMAP

Your financial journey can also be dangerous if you venture into unfamiliar territory, and it becomes even more dangerous if you don't have a good map. In 2007, the father of one of my colleagues, who was soon to retire, had all of his retirement funds in the stock market. When the dust settled after the crash of 2008, he had suffered huge losses. His intent was not to be risky with his money, but he had assumed that the stock market was the right place for his retirement assets. After the crash, the dreams he had for his retirement years changed dramatically. If my friend's father had put just half of his money into some of the secured vehicles outlined in this book, he would be smiling today with guaranteed cash flow for life.

I often encounter people who, instead of following a proven pathway, venture down rabbit trails or stumble over financial cliffs. I, too, made some wrong financial decisions in the past which cost me dearly, and my passion for the principles in this book arose out of my desire to help others avoid similar pitfalls.

Like Lewis and Clark, you need a good map. Unlike them, however, you do not need to start from scratch. Your Financial Convergence Roadmap will serve as your guide to financial safety, personal confidence and peace of mind.

TRADEOFFS

Before creating your personal Financial Convergence Roadmap, understand that every choice you make in life has trade-offs. This is certainly true with your finances. As Carl Richard said in the quote that introduced this chapter, "Being slow and steady means that you are willing to exchange the opportunity of making a killing for the assurance of never getting killed." That's a clear trade-off.

Are you willing to trade making a killing for never getting killed? If you swing for the fences every time you are up to bat, you may hit some home runs, but you will also strike out a lot more. If you focus on singles and doubles, you will hit fewer home runs but will likely win the most important ball game . . . preserving and growing assets.

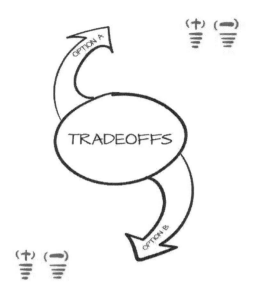

CREATING YOUR FINANCIAL CONVERGENCE ROADMAP

The focus of this chapter is to give you the tools and strategies for creating your own Financial Convergence Roadmap. I recommend that you first read through the entire book to get the full picture and then come back to this chapter to create your Roadmap.

So, let's walk through the steps. I will also include Roger and Marcia's (Chapter 2) plan as an example.

Step 1: MY FINANCIAL VALUES

Your financial values and goals are your Big River as described in Chapter 1. Everything you do financially should flow into this river. That's why Step 1 demands that you thoughtfully and carefully identify your financial values. The earlier in your financial journey that you do this, the better.

Roger and Marcia's key financial values:

- We want guaranteed lifetime income.
- We do not want to worry about the next stock market crash.
- Safety of principal is very important to us.
- Keep things simple.
- We want liquidity for emergencies and opportunities.
- We are okay with returns of 5 percent to 7 percent with no risk of losses.
- We want to minimize income taxation wherever possible.
- We want to eliminate estate taxes.
- Maximizing the inheritances to our heirs is important to us.

The worksheet on the next page is designed to simply get you started in your thinking process. Check the boxes which best identify your financial values:

Financial Values

"What's most important to me?"

Risk - Return

| Less Risk | ☐ | ☐ | ☐ | ☐ | ☐ | More Risk |

Cash Flow - Nest Egg

| More Income | ☐ | ☐ | ☐ | ☐ | ☐ | Larger Nest Egg |

Asset Management

| Auto-pilot | ☐ | ☐ | ☐ | ☐ | ☐ | Active Management |

Income Tax

| Tax on the Seed | ☐ | ☐ | ☐ | ☐ | ☐ | Tax on The Crop |

Retirement Lifestyle

| Simple, Quiet | ☐ | ☐ | ☐ | ☐ | ☐ | Active, Loud |

Financial Legacy

| Financial Legacy For Family | ☐ | ☐ | ☐ | ☐ | ☐ | Die Broke |

Income Protection

| Income Replacement Plan | ☐ | ☐ | ☐ | ☐ | ☐ | My Spouse Works More |

Step 2: MY FINANCIAL GOALS

Next, identify your key financial goals.

Roger and Marcia's key financial goals:

- Guaranteed lifetime income of $100,000/year, increasing by 3 percent per year.
- Eliminate the need to make ongoing financial decisions with our retirement assets.
- Create tax-free income on 70 percent of our retirement assets.
- Create $1,000,000 in permanent life insurance benefits for our children.
- Keep our wills and trust current.
- $100,000 minimum liquidity for emergencies or opportunities.
- Provide protection for long-term care costs.

Financial Goals

Retire at age _____

Minimum retirement income of $_____

Target retirement income of $_____

Leave a financial legacy to my heirs of $_____

Charitable giving of $_____

Other_____

_____

_____

Step 3: IDENTIFY CONVERGENT FINANCIAL STRATEGIES

Now that you have identified your key financial values and goals, select the financial strategies which best converge with those values and goals.

> Roger and Marcia's convergent financial strategies:
>
> - Use financial vehicles that do not need constant management.
> - Use financial vehicles that do not have risk of losses.
> - Use financial vehicles that are easy to understand.
> - Reposition selected assets to tax-free vehicles to achieve our 70 percent goal.
> - Work with an advisor who has experience implementing our strategies.
> - Create adequate long-term care coverage.

EXAMPLES OF FINANCIAL STRATEGIES

Here are some additional examples of financial strategies

- Reposition _____ percent of my assets into secured financial vehicles.
- Reposition _____ percent of my assets into vehicles producing tax-free income.
- Create guaranteed lifetime income no matter how long I live.
- Create more retirement income for increased travel during the early part of my retirement years.
- Maximize my qualified plans (IRA, 401(k), TSP, etc.) and take my chances on higher tax brackets during retirement.
- Pay tax on the "seed" instead of the "crop" to create tax-free income later (see Chapter 5).
- Take control of more of my money and become my own banker (see Chapter 6).
- Give my kids my values but not my money.
- Maximize the financial legacy to my heirs.
- Provide for potential long-term care needs.

- Create adequate liquidity for emergencies and opportunities.
- Create income replacement through life insurance.
- Maximize my charitable giving.

THE FINANCIAL STRATEGIES WHICH BEST CONVERGE WITH
MY GOALS AND VALUES ARE:

1. _____

_____

2. _____

_____

3. _____

_____

4. _____

_____

5. _____

_____

Step 4: CONVERGENT FINANCIAL VEHICLES

The fourth step in creating your Financial Convergence Roadmap is to choose the financial vehicles which best converge with your values, goals, and strategies.

Adam and Bob are over-the-road truckers. Both originate in Billings, Montana. Both are headed for St. Louis, Missouri. Adam is hauling horses. Bob's freight is farm equipment. Both are doing the same thing (trucking) and both have the same destination (St. Louis), but the vehicles they use will differ greatly. Smart truckers use the vehicle which is best suited to the freight being hauled.

In a similar way, the financial vehicles that Adam chooses may be different from those used by Bob. Let's say, for example, that Adam's key financial goal is to create maximum retirement income with minimum risk. Bob, on the other hand, has a substantial defined benefit pension plan and his top financial goal is to maximize the transfer of his financial assets to his heirs at death. Different goals (freight) requires different vehicles.

So, the question is not, "Which financial vehicles are good and which are bad" but rather, "Which financial vehicles best converge with my financial values, goals and strategies?"

A flatbed works well for hauling farm machinery but not so well for horses.

Roger and Marcia's convergent financial vehicles:

- High cash value Indexed Universal Life Insurance
- Survivorship Life Insurance
- Indexed Annuities that focus on maximizing future income
- Lake property with Low-management

INVENTORY OF FINANCAL VEHICLES

Below is an inventory of several financial vehicles. I have ranked each of them in five different areas. The rankings are mine and are general in nature. The purpose is to help you identify which financial vehicles converge with your values, goals and strategies. **Ranking: 1 = Low. 5 = High**

VEHICLE	RISK TO PRINCIPAL?	TAX ADVANTAGE?	INCOME TOOL?	MGMT REQUIRED?	LEGACY TOOL?
Bank Savings	1	1	1	1	1
Bank CD	1	1	1	1	1
Muni Bonds	2	5	1	2	1
Corp. Bonds	3	1	1	2	1
Fixed Annuity	1	3	3	1	3
Indexed Annuity	1	3	5	1	4
Variable Annuity	5	3	3	5	2
Participating Whole Life	1	5	3	1	5
IUL - Index Univ. Life	1	5	5	1	5
FPCM	1	1	4	1	3
REIT	3	1	3	3	3
Inv. RE	3	3	5	3	5
Mutual Funds	4	3	3	5	3
Individual Stocks	4	3	2	5	3

Precious Metals	4	3	2	3	3
Business Ownership	1-5	3	1-5	5	5

THE FINANCIAL VEHICLES WHICH BEST CONVERGE WITH MY GOALS, VALUES AND STRATEGIES ARE:

1. _____

2. _____

3. _____

4. _____

5. _____

PUTTING IT ALL TOGETHER

You have now identified your **financial values** to guide your financial decisions going forward, and you have listed your key **financial goals** that are in harmony with your financial values. In your Financial Convergence Roadmap, your financial values and financial goals become your Big River.

Financial Convergence is created as you identify the tributaries—the **financial strategies and financial vehicles**—which best converge into your Big River.

FINANCIAL CONVERGENCE ROADMAP®
PLANNING TOOL
"MY BIG RIVER"

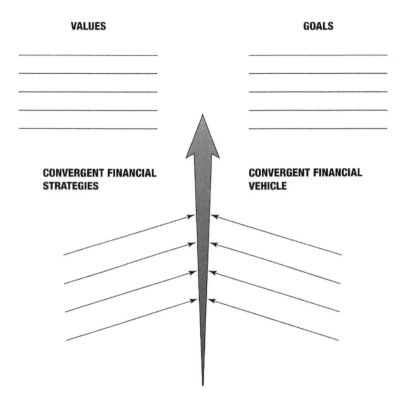

VALUES

GOALS

CONVERGENT FINANCIAL STRATEGIES

CONVERGENT FINANCIAL VEHICLE

CONVERGENCE AT THE CORE:

- A good Financial Convergence Roadmap is essential for a successful financial journey.
- Every financial decision has trade-offs.
- It all starts with clarifying your financial values and goals.
- Your completed Financial Convergence Roadmap will become a valuable financial tool over your lifetime.

WHAT'S NEXT?

In Section 2, **Resources**, we will showcase financial strategies designed to help you **create more income with less risk.**

PART 2:

RESOURCES

4

Index Your Way
to Wealth

"Money is hard to earn and easy to lose. Guard yours with care"

Brian Tracy

Mary heard one of my radio ads on growing money without risk of losses and called for an appointment. Single and age 55, she was concerned about adequate money for retirement. I asked questions and listened carefully to her

answers. Her story was not pretty. She had built
up her IRA to $100,000 eight years ago. When we
talked, it was worth $27,000.

Another story of trusting Wall Street and another
story of "Now, what do I do?"

If only she had understood our financial
convergence principles 10 years earlier and had
created a Financial Convergence Roadmap. The
financial values she shared with me included
safety of principal, but her financial strategies
did not converge with those values. If she had
used the indexing strategies outlined in this
chapter, her account value today would be
around $200,000 instead of $27,000.

UNDERSTANDING INDEXING

Indexing is simple, yet powerful. It allows you to
receive good returns without the risk of stock
market losses. With Indexing, you mirror the
market without being in the market. In the UP
years, you have gains; in the DOWN years, your
gains are locked in with no risk of losses. **Your
account trajectory is North or East but never
South!**

INDEXING ROADMAP

NORTH OR EAST.....NEVER SOUTH!

The type of indexing to which I am referring is done by life insurance companies in either an Indexed Universal Life policy (Chapter 5) or a Fixed Index Annuity (Chapter 7). Do not confuse this strategy with an index fund, which is a type of mutual fund portfolio designed to track a market index such as the S & P 500. An index fund still has risk of losses; the type of indexing outlined here does not.

Reflect for a moment on how it would feel to go to sleep every night knowing that your hard-earned retirement assets will produce gains in the years when the stock market index (S & P 500 Index, Barclay's, Russell 2000, etc.) is up, but when there are losses, or worse, crashes like 1987, 2001, or 2008, and ???, your cash values do not suffer these losses (zero is your hero). Sound too good to be true? **In a moment, I will show you that it is both very good and very true.**

WALL STREET MIND VIRUS

Have you ever heard this one? "Don't worry much about stock market losses when you are younger. You have lots of time to recover." If you are indoctrinated with the same propaganda long enough, you begin to believe it. I have heard people use the term "mind viruses" to describe this phenomenon and the Wall Street influenza can be very contagious – and costly.

The truth is, the younger you are when stock market losses occur, the more you lose. Please understand that when you lose money in the stock market, that money is gone forever. If your account "recovers," it does not recover the money you lost. It simply has gains on the amount remaining after the losses.

The below example proves my point:

Stock Market Loss @ age 40:	**$40,000**
Retirement Age:	**65**
Years Until Retirement:	**25**
Assumed Growth Rate:	**7%**
Lost opportunity on $40,000 over 25 years @ 7%:	**$217,093**
Assumed Years in Retirement: 20	
Cost of Lost Opportunity @ age 85:	**$840,000**

Here's another important truth about stock market losses:

If your stock market account loses:	Here's the gains just to get back to even:
20%	25%
30%	43%
40%	67%
50%	100%

HOW INDEXING WORKS

So how does indexing in an indexed life policy or indexed annuity actually work? How do I capture the upside of the stock market index without the downside risk? How does my account value hold in the years when the stock market tanks?

An Overview of How Indexing Works

Let's use a hypothetical $1,000 year premium. When your premium is applied to your plan, the company separates it into two parts:

Part A: Approximately $950 goes into the life insurance company's General Account Portfolio. This account is made up of conservative, safe investments. At the end of a year, the $950 is back to $1,000.

Part B: Approximately $50 is used to purchase options. These options will provide a return on your money equal to the annual increase in the selected Index (S & P 500 Index, Barclay's Index, etc.) up to an annual cap if applicable.

Results:

• Down market: Your $950 grows back to the $1,000.
• Up market: Your account grows based on the growth of the index.

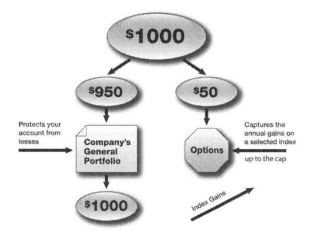

- Approximately five percent of your premiums are used to purchase options tied to a specific index.
- The other 95 percent or so goes into the life insurance company's general account, which is boring (remember, boring is good when it comes to your retirement assets!). It chugs along at about 5 percent year-in and year-out. At the end of the policy year, your $950 is back to $1,000.
- The option is tied to a specific index (S & P 500, Russell 2000, Barclays, NASDAQ, etc.)
- This diagram assumes that we are using an annual point-to-point strategy. (monthly strategies are also available with some carriers along with 2 and 3-year point-to-point strategies).
- If the index has gains during the policy year, the option contract that was purchased guarantees gains on your entire cash value for that year. Some indexed vehicles have caps on the topside, others do not. In the years when the index has gains, your account value goes north.

- If the index has losses in a given policy year, the option is not used. In these years, your $950 in the company's general account will be back to $1,000 at the end of the contract year. In the years when the index has losses, your account value goes east, but not south.
- So, in a year when the index is down, your cash values do not suffer these losses. You hold the value of your account at its high-water mark, minus any policy fees and insurance cost.
- The result is that you capture the upside of the market without the downside risk.

Note: The above indexing strategy is done by the life insurance company. Most carriers have several index options and allow you to make changes in the index or indexes that you use. So, go on vacation, enjoy your retirement years and don't worry about the stock market losing your hard-earned money.

Remember, if don't suffer stock market losses, you do not have to hit home runs to do very well with your money! Singles and doubles win ball games.

THE POWER OF THE ANNUAL RESET

The markets are getting more volatile with increasing natural disasters, worldwide geopolitical unrest and recurring asset bubbles. And the likelihood of continued market volatility appears almost certain.

Here's the good news. With the annual reset in an indexed vehicle, market volatility can become your friend if you own an indexed universal life or indexed annuity.

Here's why.

Each year, on the anniversary date of your policy, the index is reset. Let's say that the index you are using is the S & P 500 and your policy anniversary date is January 1 of each year.

On January 1, 2008, the S & P 500 Index was at
1,379. On January 1, 2009, it was at 866; a 38%
loss[4]. During the crash year of 2008, you did not
have any gains in your indexed vehicle, BUT, you
also did not have any losses! Then on January 1,
2009, your Index benchmark is reset to 866. This
means that future index gains are now based on
the growth from this lower reset amount. So,
during the next years as the S & P 500 recovered,
you capture the gains based on the lower reset S &
P amount of 866, not 1,379.

INDEX RESET EXAMPLE:

1/1/08   S & P 500 Index = 1,379

1/1/09   S & P 500 Index = 866

- During 2008, if your money was in the S & P
  500 Index, you lost 38% of your account
  value. You now need 61% gains just to get
  back to even.
- If your money was in an indexed life or
  indexed annuity, you had no market losses.
- Then, on January 1, 2009, all the future gains
  in your indexed vehicle are based on the
  lower reset S & P 500 amount of 866.

THE POWER IN THE ANNUAL RESET

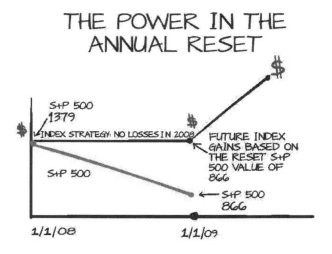

HISTORY LESSON

The following graph shows actual returns from the 17- year period of 1998 through 2015. Line #1 is a fixed 5% annual return, line #2 is the S & P 500 Index, and line #3 is the Index strategy with a 12% annual cap.

COMPARISON: 1998 – 2015

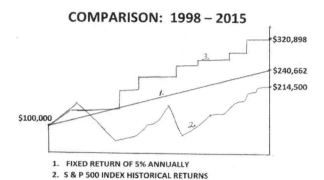

1. FIXED RETURN OF 5% ANNUALLY
2. S & P 500 INDEX HISTORICAL RETURNS
3. INDEX STRATEGY WITH A 12% ANNUAL CAP

The way I look at it, your retirement assets should be sacred ground and not blown around by the whims and quirks of Wall Street. Unfortunately, many people do not realize that there is a better way. Maybe you were one of them, but not anymore.

CONVERGENCE AT THE CORE:

- Watch out for the Wall Street "mind viruses."
- Indexing produces growth in up years and no losses in down years.
- With the annual reset, indexing can be your friend in volatile markets.
- If you never have a loss, you don't need huge returns to do very well with your money.
- Singles and doubles win ball games.
- If you lose 38% like in the 2008 crash, you need gains of 61% just to get back to even.

WHAT'S NEXT?

In the next chapter, we will discuss which is better - **paying tax on the seed or on the crop?** Don't miss this one.

5

Seed or Crop?

We shall tax and tax, and spend and spend, and elect and elect.

Harry Hopkins.

TAX THE SEED OR THE CROP?

I was born and raised on a beef cattle farm in central Minnesota. With a big herd of Registered Polled Hereford cattle, we grew a lot of corn. It always amazed me how the small bags of seed planted in the spring could produce huge truckloads of corn in the fall.

So, picture my dad heading to the field one sunny spring morning on his International Harvester 560 tractor with an eight-row corn planter in tow. A car drives up and a man in a suit and tie jumps out. "Hi Oren, I am your friendly IRS agent and I have two options for you on your income taxes. You can pay me tax on these bags of seed here or you can pay me tax on the semi loads of crop in the fall. What's your pick?"

My dad was not only a hard-working farmer, but he was quick on his feet. Without hesitation, he replied, "I will go with the tax on the seed, thank you."

SEED OR CROP?

BIGGEST RISK TO YOUR RETIREMENT ASSETS?

David Walker, former Comptroller General of the United States as well as the head of the Government Accountability Office had a commentary for CNN back in 2009, entitled, "Why Your Taxes Could Double."[5] In the article, he outlined why, given our national debt and the propensity for Washington D. C. to spend billions above its income, it would not be unreasonable to think that our taxes could double in the future.

Pretty stark.

So how have we done since Walker's statement in 2009?

The national debt has skyrocketed
Entitlements continue to escalate,
Spending in Washington, DC is out of control.

Anyone who dares to use a little common sense knows that the current path is unsustainable. Something has to give. Most likely it will be you and me.

TAX CODE 7702 TO THE RESCUE

7702 is a "sweet spot" in the monster tax code. Even though 7702 has been around for a long time, most people are not aware of how it works . . . or how powerful it is.

The good news is that 7702 is available to everyone, not just the mega-wealthy.

Code section IRC 7702 outlines the income tax regulations on cash value life insurance.[6] In summary, 7702 provides tax-deferred accumulation on policy cash values, tax-free access to your principal (cost basis) and tax-free availability of your total cash values through properly structured policy loans (more about loans in the next chapter).

COMPARISON

The following chart compares paying tax on the crop (stock market/mutual fund 401(k), IRA, etc.) vs. paying tax on the seed using an Indexed Universal Life policy. The comparison assumes no tax increases in the future. If future taxes increase, the difference is even more dramatic.

Take special notice of the last number: **$1,201,974.** Looks like my dad made the right choice! And this is assuming that the 401(k)/IRA stock market account has a gross return of 8% with 2% fees and with no losses over the entire 55-year period!

SO, WHICH DO YOU

WANT TO PAY TAX ON . . .

SEED OR CROP?

	401(k) or IRA Stocks/MF	INDEXED UNIVERSAL LIFE
ANNUAL CONTRIBUTION	$7,500	$5,025
CONTRIBUTION YEARS	25	25
ASSUMED RATE OF RETURN	8% Gross	7% Gross
GROSS AMOUNT WITHDRAWN ANNUALLY @ 65	$70,610	$47,309
INCOME TAX ON WITHDRAWALS	$23,301	$0
NET AMOUNT RECEIVED PER YEAR	**$47,309**	**$47,309**
YEARS THE PRINCIPAL WILL LAST	**19**	**35+**
TOTAL AMOUNT RECEIVED	$898,871	$1,655,815
DEATH BENEFIT @ AGE 100	$0	$445,030
TOTAL RECEIVED PLUS DEATH BENEFIT	$898,871	$2,100,845
DIFFERENCE IN TOTAL PAYOUT		**$1,201,974**

Assumptions on the above comparison:

- Indexed Universal Life Policy
  - Male, age 35, Preferred Non-smoker
  - Underwritten by a specific U. S. Life Insurance carrier
- Income Taxes
  - 33% marginal bracket – combined state and federal
  - No future increase in tax bracket
- Stock Market Account Returns
  - Stock market account has a gross annual return of 8% with 2% average fees.
  - No stock market losses over the entire 55- year period!
- Indexed Universal Life Returns
  - 7% average index returns
  - All fees and costs are included
  - 5% loan interest rate

ASSET ALLOCATION ANALYSIS

Don't put your head in the sand when it comes to paying taxes on your retirement income. It is going to happen and it could get ugly. Being proactive now could save you thousands later on.

What is your asset allocation plan? No, I am not talking about market risk allocations. Yes, that is important and needs your attention. However, the asset allocation plan to which I am referring is **income tax allocation.** This could be your greatest retirement income risk.

What are your current portfolio allocations for income tax risk? What percent of your retirement portfolio is subject to income tax risk? Do a quick analysis using the following chart:

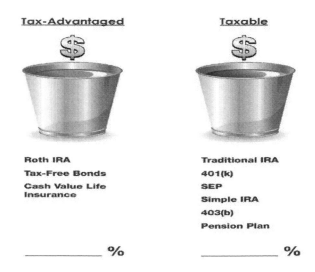

Asset Allocation Analysis

<u>Tax-Advantaged</u>

Roth IRA
Tax-Free Bonds
Cash Value Life
Insurance

_____ %

<u>Taxable</u>

Traditional IRA
401(k)
SEP
Simple IRA
403(b)
Pension Plan

_____ %

What did you come up with? How much of your retirement income will be taxable? The majority of people who come to me for guidance have nearly 100% of their retirement assets in the tax-risk bucket. Does that describe you? So, what happens to your retirement plan if tax brackets increase 50% during your retirement years? That would be like taking a 50% hit on your stock market account over-and-over again. Sound like fun?

Here's another myth: I will be in a lower tax bracket when I retire.

The truth is that most of the deductions during your working years are greatly reduced or have disappeared in retirement:

- Mortgage interest deduction
- Qualified Plan contributions
- Work-related deductions
- Dependents (children) exemptions
- Investment property depreciation and deductions

How would you feel if your gross retirement income of $150,000 per year shrinks to $75,000 after Mr. Tax Man gets done with you? Half of your income or more going to taxes? Could that be possible? Absolutely. That is why Ed Slott, CPA, best-selling author and national tax experts says in his book, *The Retirement Savings Time Bomb and How to Diffuse It*, **"Taxes are your single biggest retirement risk."**[7]

Taxes are a huge enemy to your wealth. Know how to use the right weapons to fight them off.

TAX REALLOCATION PLANNING - HOW TO PAY TAX ON THE SEED

There are three primary ways to pay tax on the seed.

- Tax-Free Municipal Bonds
- Roth IRA's
- Cash-Value Life Insurance

My choice of the three is high cash value life insurance. Here's why:

- Stronger historical returns than tax-free bonds (when the IUL policy is designed properly).
- Greater retirement cash flow potential.
- Enhanced security of your principal (A 100-year old A+ rated life insurance company has been one of the safest places for your retirement assets).
- Increased control over your money.
- Freedom from the Roth restrictions on contributions and withdrawals.

INDEXED UNIVERSAL LIFE (IUL) - CUSTOMIZE AND WIN BIG:

An Indexed Universal Life Policy enables you to pay tax on the seed, not the crop. It is a financial vehicle with powerful benefits. Do these features and benefits converge with your financial values and goals?

- Potential double-digit gains in the years when the market index has growth
- Safety of Principal – When the index has down years, zero is your hero.
- Historical average returns of 7% or better with the top carriers
- Tax-deferred growth
- Tax-advantaged income (through properly designed policy loans)
- Liquidity for emergencies and opportunities
- Control of your money
- Become your own banker (see Chapter 6)
- Tax-free death benefits to heirs
- Good wealth transfer tool
- Creditor protection (rules vary state-by-state)

The Power of The
Indexed Universal Life Policy

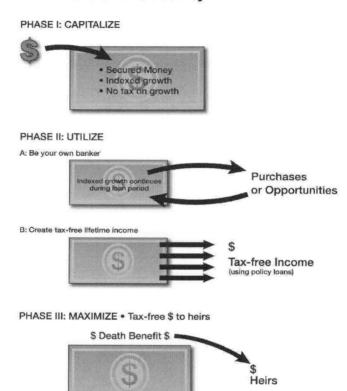

PHASE I: CAPITALIZE

- Secured Money
- Indexed growth
- No tax on growth

PHASE II: UTILIZE

A: Be your own banker

Indexed growth continues during loan period

Purchases or Opportunities

B: Create tax-free lifetime income

$
Tax-free Income
(using policy loans)

PHASE III: MAXIMIZE • Tax-free $ to heirs

$ Death Benefit $

$
Heirs

HOWEVER, AND THIS IS IMPORTANT . . .

The Indexed Universal Life policy needs to be properly custom designed to maximize tax-advantaged future income and minimize fees.

Like most things, you can find a bunch of negative stuff on the internet regarding Indexed Universal Life. Actually a lot of it could be true when policies are not designed properly.

Find an Indexed Universal Life Insurance specialist to help you. These specialists know how to properly design your policy within the 7702 IRS tax guidelines, enabling you to maximize both your accumulation and distributions.

WHOLE LIFE OR INDEXED UNIVERSAL LIFE . . . WHICH IS BETTER?

Good question. The answer is "both" or "it all depends."

If your goal is creating the maximum tax-advantaged retirement income, IUL is my product of choice. Its flexible design and historical indexing returns favor it for greater future cash flow.

If your goal is creating the maximum paid up life insurance as an estate transfer tool, a participating whole life policy from a top carrier is the best fit.

Both Indexed Universal Life and whole life policies provide attractive "be your own banker" features outlined in the next chapter.

CONVERGENCE AT THE CORE:

- Income taxes may be the biggest risk to your retirement assets.
- Pay tax on the seed or pay tax on the crop? It's your choice.
- Tax Code 7702 provides powerful income tax advantages.
- Asset allocation analysis must include both risk analysis and income tax analysis.
- Cash value life insurance, designed correctly, is a great tool for creating tax advantaged retirement income.

WHAT'S NEXT?

In the next chapter, we will show you how to **become your own banker** and use the strategies that the wealthy have been using for decades.

PART 2: RESOURCES

6

Bank on Yourself

"It's not how much money you make, but how much money you keep, how hard it works for you, and for how many generations you keep it."

Robert Kiyosaki

LEARN FROM THE WEALTHY

Wealthy people love cash value life insurance and they have been reaping its benefits for decades. Ask J. C. Penney or Walt Disney or Doris Christopher (founder of The Pampered Chef) or Ray

Kroc (founder of McDonalds). Each one has a compelling story of how he or she used the "bank on yourself" features of cash value life insurance to help launch their multi-million dollar enterprises.

BECOME A CONTROL FREAK AND WIN BIG

How much of your money is truly in your control? If a unique opportunity presented itself today where you needed $100,000 to double your money quickly in a secured environment, could you do it? Opportunities are out there and some of them even come running your way. But to take advantage, in almost every case, you need seed money. You need money that you control and can access quickly when those opportunities arise.

Do you control your 401(k)? Do you control your IRA? Can you access money from either of those accounts without penalties or taxes? What percent of your financial assets do you truly control? If you want to be on the same playing field as the wealthy, start designing a game plan where you control your money.

OPEN YOUR OWN BANK

A high cash value life insurance policy is one financial vehicle where you have control. And, once established, it will become your personal bank providing opportunities throughout your lifetime.

But establishing your personal bank doesn't happen overnight.

Phase 1: Capitalize. This is the hardest phase because it takes discipline, patience and fighting against the uninformed naysayers. It is a lot like flying a commercial airplane where the biggest burn on fuel is in takeoff. On shorter flights, as much as 25 percent of the fuel on a commercial airliner is used just for takeoff. Once at cruising altitude, the fuel usage becomes much more efficient.

Capitalizing your cash value life insurance "bank" works in a similar way. The most "fuel" (fees) are on the front end. Then, assuming it is designed correctly, the longer you own the policy, the more efficient and powerful it becomes.

Phase 2: Utilize. With a properly designed policy, you should be able to start down the road to "banking on yourself" in year two or three. Now, rather than going to the traditional lenders, you go to your own "bank" and use the cash values in your policy to finance cars, business equipment, vacations, college, etc. And when financial opportunities come your way, you are prepared to take advantage.

Phase 3: Income-ize (yes, a new word). So, you are now at retirement age. And over the years you have used your "bank" to finance lots of things. You have also been a good banker and paid back all the loans, and maybe even used a little higher interest rate than the bank charges, since the interest is going back into **your bank** and not the one in the brick building down the street.

Here in Phase 3, your cash value policy, used correctly, becomes a tax-free retirement income machine. What if former Comptroller General, David Walker, is right and Income tax rates double in the future? What if it takes $150,000 withdrawals from your 401(k) or IRA to end up with $75,000 after taxes? That's when you will be smiling every time you make a tax-advantaged retirement income withdrawal from your cash value life insurance program.

Phase 4: Maximize. And when your life here is over, the tax-free policy loans that you used for retirement income are paid back with a portion of your death benefits. The remaining death benefit goes tax-free to your heirs, creating a financial legacy.

YOU FINANCE EVERYTHING YOU BUY

"You finance everything you buy." says Nelson Nash, in his book, *Infinite Banking*.[8] Think about that statement for a minute. With every purchase, you either pay interest to a lending entity (bank, credit union, credit card company, individual, etc.) for the use of their money, or you give up its earning potential by using your own money. So, everything you buy is financed, either by paying someone else to use their money or by losing the earning you could have captured when you use your own money.

HOW INDEXED LIFE POLICY LOANS WORK

Now what if you could use someone else's money, pay him five percent, then place that borrowed money in a secured environment at seven percent. Would you do it? With the right cash value policy, you can create just such a program.

So, let's talk about how the policy loans work. The first thing you need to know is that there are two types of policy loans: direct recognition loans and non-direct recognition loans. It is important that you work with a life insurance company that uses non-direct recognition loans. In a non-direct recognition loan environment, you are borrowing money from the life insurance company using your cash value as collateral. In this model, your entire cash value continues to receive the indexed returns or annual dividends just as if no policy loan had been taken.

As an example, let's say that the cash value in your Indexed Universal Life policy is $200,000. You take a loan of $125,000 and pay five percent interest to the life insurance company on the loan. In a non-direct recognition loan environment, your full

$200,000 continues to receive the indexed returns just as if there was no loan.

So, if, over time, the indexed returns average seven percent annually, your policy cash value would be receiving two percent more than the interest rate charged on your loan (seven percent minus five percent). We would call this a two percent positive arbitrage (pronounced **Ahr**-bi-trahzh). Could the index returns be less than a seven percent average? Sure. But historically, indexed universal life policies have done around seven percent or better on the cash value crediting when using the top companies and the right indexing strategies.

In a direct recognition loan environment and using the same example as above, only $75,000 ($200,000 minus the $125,000 loan) would continue to receive the full indexing or dividend returns to your cash value and you lose all opportunity for the positive arbitrage.

Need a car loan? When you have built up adequate cash value, simply go to your "personal bank" involving no forms, questions, hassles, or delays. You just make a phone call and the funds are transferred to your account. Then as your own banker, you repay the loan back into your policy over the time frame that you choose.

One way to be a good banker is to research the comparable loan interest rates at the bank down the street and pay the loan back (to your "bank") at a little higher rate – while at the same time creating more reserves for your next opportunity.

Check out this auto loan comparison:

USUAL WAY	BANK ON MYSELF

Borrow $30,000 from the bank.
7% interest rate paid to the bank
$594 monthly payment
Total to the bank: $35,640
Sell car for $14,000
(end of year 5)

Borrow $30,000 from my policy
7% interest rate paid to my policy
$594 monthly payment
Total to my policy: $35,640
Sell car for $14,000
(end of year 5)

RESULTS:
$14,000 Available for next purchase

RESULTS:
$49,640 Available for next purchase

CONVERGENCE AT THE CORE:

- Wealthy people love cash value life insurance.
- Control of your money can create huge financial opportunities over your lifetime.
- You finance everything you buy.
- Become your own banker and win big.
- Use life insurance companies that provide non-direct recognition loans.

WHAT'S NEXT?

In the next chapter, we will show you how to create **secure, guaranteed lifetime income,** even if you live to be age 100 or more.

PART 2: RESOURCES

7

Income for a Lifetime

"Investing should be more like
watching paint dry or watching grass
grow. If you want excitement, take
$800 and go to Las Vegas."

Paul Samuelson

Randy and Susan came to one of my seminars; after
hearing my presentation, they requested a
personal appointment to talk further. They had
been burned in the past by the stock market and

were looking for ideas for how to maximize retirement income without risk of losses.

Over the years, Randy and Susan had put a lot of money into mutual fund accounts. During one of our early conversations, I asked them what their returns had averaged on their mutual fund accounts over the past 15 years. They acknowledged that they had no idea. So, after gathering the necessary information, I did some simple math and found that they had averaged only a two percent annual ROI on these accounts over the past 15 years.

What have the returns been on your mutual fund accounts? If you are like most people that I encounter, you also may not know the answer. I strongly suggest that you find out. A two percent return on risk money is not good. A Wall Street Journal article on May 9, 2014, stated that the average annual returns for individual investors in stocks/mutual funds over the past 30 years has been 3.7 percent per year.[9]

The financial resource that we will discuss in this chapter, a Fixed Index Annuity, is one of the vehicles that Randy and Susan decided to incorporate into their Financial Convergence Roadmap.

HOW TO NEVER RUN OUT OF MONEY!

In Chapter 3, we showed you how to create your Financial Convergence Roadmap by first identifying your financial values and goals and then choosing the financial strategies and vehicles to best converge with those values and goals.

If one of your key goals is to know for certain that you will never run out of money no matter how long you live, this chapter is for you.

Life Insurance and annuity companies are designed to provide guarantees. Your stock market account is not. A life insurance company's annuity can guarantee lifetime income; your stock market account cannot.

Just as life insurance death benefits are there to protect against dying too soon, annuities are designed to protect against living too long.

Phil and Ross

Phil and Ross are both 10 years from retirement. Both have $400,000 in their IRAs. Phil is tired of worrying about what's going to happen with the stock market. He says, "What if it crashes again like 2008 when I am a year from retirement?" Ross, on the other hand, is more of a risk taker with his retirement account and seems to enjoy the thrill of the ride like the roller-coasters at Disney. Ross may change his tune in a few years, however.

For Phil, a Fixed Index Annuity could be a great choice. Here's why. Let's assume that the index growth on Phil's annuity has future performance equal to that of the past 10 years with a specific top-tier annuity carrier.

Based on those assumptions, when Phil retires in 10 years, the annual income generated from his $400,000 IRA would be $42,030. Each subsequent year when the underlying index has growth, his income will lock in at a higher amount. In addition, Phil has a guarantee in his contract that he will never run out of money no matter how long he lives and even if his account value goes to zero!

LET'S COMPARE

What stock market/mutual fund returns would Ross need to create the same income, assuming his stock market advisor is like most and recommends that he withdraw 4 percent per year of his account value in retirement?

<u>Ross would need a return of 10 percent net (after fees) with no losses to equal Phil's initial income.</u>

Could 10 percent net after fees with no losses occur? Yes, it could happen, but not very likely. The value of the S & P 500 on January 1, 2000 was 1425.51. Sixteen years later, on January 1, 2016, the value was 1918.60. If you calculate the annual returns, including reinvestment of dividends, you are at 3.8% per year. This means that If Ross invested $100,000 into the S & P 500 index on January 1, 2000, his account value 16 years later would be approximately $181,605 on January 1, 2016.[10] Again, that's an average annual return of less than four percent during the first 16 years of this millennium. After fees, his return will likely be around three percent or less. That's a long way from a 10 percent net return needed. Even worse,

Ross could experience a stock market crash a year or two before retirement.

That's why Phil loves his Indexed Income Annuity and sleeps well at night!

CHOOSING THE RIGHT ANNUITY

When you shop for a new car, you likely compile your short list of important features, styles, makes, and models. Then you test drive several that fit your list, negotiate the price, and make the deal. Without your short list before starting your search, you would likely be overwhelmed and frustrated with 263 different choices - the number of different cars sold in the USA in 2016. That's a lot of windshield time.

The same is true in the annuity world, only more so. There are more than 800 life insurance companies in the USA and most of them sell annuities, each with several choices. **So how do you choose the best annuity for you from a list of several thousand?**

HERE'S HOW TO QUICKLY NARROW THE FIELD:

1. Begin by selecting only the life insurance companies that have longevity, strong ratings and good reserves.
2. Select the companies that sell fixed index annuity products. There are three general types of annuities: Fixed, Variable, and Indexed. If you are looking for good returns without risk of losses, I recommend a fixed index annuity.
3. Select the annuities that can create increasing lifetime income each year the underlying index has growth.
4. Find the fixed index annuity products that are focused on maximizing your lifetime income without having to annuitize.

When you follow these four steps, the field of thousands is reduced to a handful. Any annuity that makes the cut on these four requirements should be a good fit for you.

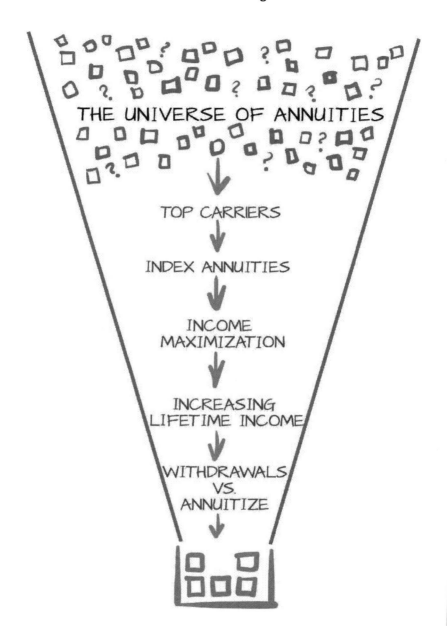

THE UNIVERSE OF ANNUITIES

TOP CARRIERS

INDEX ANNUITIES

INCOME MAXIMIZATION

INCREASING LIFETIME INCOME

WITHDRAWALS VS. ANNUITIZE

FIXED INDEX ANNUITY 101

CREATORS: Annuities are created by life insurance companies. You can't get your stock market account to birth an annuity.

PHASES: Annuities have two phases: an **Accumulation Phase** and a **Distribution Phase.** Sounds simple. But it gets a bit more interesting in knowing how best to accumulate and how to best distribute.

- **Accumulation Phase.** The accumulation design of an indexed annuity works in much the same way as an Indexed Universal Life policy: gains in the UP years, no losses in the DOWN years. Annuity carriers and policies will vary regarding caps on the annual growth, bonuses on the income values, and options for how to receive your lifetime income.

- **Distribution Phase.** You have two basic options: **Annuitize your cash value or take income withdrawals from your cash value.**

Annuitize: Here you make a trade with the life insurance company. You give them the cash in your annuity and they give you an income for a certain number of years or for your lifetime. Once the trade is agreed to and signed, you only have access to the stream of income and no longer to your cash account.

Withdrawals: The second option on distributions (the one which I generally recommend) is to keep your cash value and set up lifetime withdrawals. This provides more flexibility in case you need a chunk of cash later.

ANNUITIZE

VS.

WITHDRAWALS

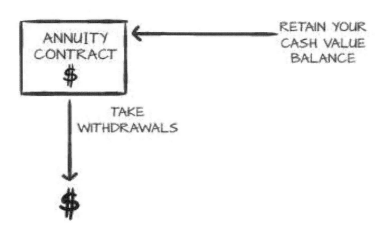

TAXES: Your taxes are deferred until you begin withdrawals. If your annuity is in a Traditional IRA, 100 percent of withdrawals are reported as income like any Traditional IRA investment. If your annuity is a non-IRA (we call that non-qualified money), the earnings portion of your withdrawals are taxable. The money you have contributed (called your cost basis) will not be taxed again. When you make withdrawals, you pay tax on the gains first (LIFO = last in, first out).

CONVERGENCE AT THE CORE:

- Do you know what your net returns have been on your stock market/mutual fund accounts? If not, why not?
- What kind of returns will you need in your stock market/mutual fund account to equal the income that a good Fixed Index Annuity will provide?

WHAT'S NEXT?

In the next chapter, **I will show you how to avoid the disaster of being forced to make withdrawals from your stock market account when the market is down.**

PART 2: RESOURCES

8

Two Buckets

113

"An investment in knowledge
pays the best interest."
Benjamin Franklin

Growing up on a beef cattle farm in central
Minnesota, my brothers and I spent a lot of time
taking care of our herd of Registered Polled
Hereford cattle. We would feed the corn silage and
then follow up with a "dessert" of ground corn and
oats. Carrying two buckets of the corn and oats,
even though there was more total weight, was

easier than using just one bucket because the two buckets balanced the weight on both sides of my body.

Balance is important in many areas of life, not just in feeding cattle. One place where balance can prove extremely valuable is with your retirement income "buckets."

To demonstrate, let's examine the retirement accounts for **"One-Bucket Brian"** and **"Two-Bucket Benjamin."** Today, Both Brian and Benjamin are age 80 and both began withdrawals from their retirement accounts fifteen years ago at age 66. When they began retirement withdrawals, each had total retirement assets of $1,500,000 and they each withdrew $100,000 per year with a 1% inflation increase each year. So, everything was the same, except the balance of their asset buckets.

One-Bucket Brian has 100 percent of his retirement money in the stock market. All his retirement eggs were in one bucket. Why? Because his advisor has convinced him that riding the ups and downs of the stock market will be fine, telling him "Don't worry about the ups and downs . . . it will all work out over time."

Two-Bucket Benjamin's advisor, on the other hand, recommended he establish two buckets for his retirement assets, one stock market bucket and the other an indexed IUL bucket or an Indexed Annuity bucket. These assets are secure when the stock market takes a nose dive.

The following two charts show the year-by-year numbers for Brian and Benjamin. The results may surprise you.

ASSUMPTIONS:

- Both stock market accounts are in the S & P 500 Index Fund with returns equal to the actual performance over the past 15 years.
- The assets for Benjamin's Bucket #2 are in an Indexed Universal Life plan with average index returns of 7%.
- In the years when the S & P 500 Index had losses (years 1 and 7), Benjamin made income withdrawals from his Indexed Life plan.

ONE-BUCKET BRIAN

One Bucket Brian's Retirement Account

$1,500,000 Stock Market Account				
Age	Historical S & P 500 Index Returns	Beginning Year Balance	Annual Withdrawals	Year Ending Balance
66	-22.1%	1,500,000	100,000	1,090,600
67	28.7%	1,090,600	101,000	1,273,615
68	10.9%	1,273,615	102,010	1,299,310
69	4.9%	1,299,310	103,030	1,254,897
70	15.8%	1,254,897	104,060	1,332,670
71	5.5%	1,332,670	105,101	1,295,085
72	-37.0%	1,295,085	106,152	749,028
73	26.5%	749,028	107,213	811,895
74	15.1%	811,895	108,285	809,856
75	2.1%	809,856	109,368	715,198
76	16.0%	715,198	110,462	701,494
77	32.4%	701,494	111,506	781,065
78	13.7%	781,065	112,682	759,951
79	1.4%	759,951	113,809	655,188
80	12.0%	655,188	114,947	605,070

TWO-BUCKET BENJAMIN

 **AND**

	$1,200,000 Stock Market Account					$300,000 IUL Account		Total
Age	Historical SVP 500 Index Returns	Beginning. Year Balance	Annual Withdrawal	Ending Year Balance	Death Benefit	Annual Withdrawal	End Year Cash Value	Total Retirement Value
66	-22.1%	1,200,000	0	934,800	151,025	100,000	217,623	1,152,423
67	28.7%	934,800	101,000	1,073,100	154,554	0	236,163	1,309,263
68	10.9%	1,073,100	102,010	1,076,939	158,123	0	256,252	1,333,191
69	4.9%	1,076,939	103,030	1,021,631	161,724	0	278,011	1,299,642
70	15.8%	1,021,631	104,060	1,062,547	165,352	0	301,568	1,364,115
71	5.5%	1,062,547	105,101	1,010,105	169,001	0	327,072	1,337,177
72	-37.0%	1,010,105	0	636,366	58,525	106,152	242,033	878,399
73	26.5%	636,366	107,213	669,379	53,788	0	265,136	934,515
74	15.1%	669,379	108,285	645,819	48,621	0	290,441	936,260
75	2.1%	645,819	109,368	547,717	43,001	0	318,168	865,885
76	16.0%	547,717	110,462	507,215	36,865	0	348,497	855,712
77	32.4%	507,215	111,506	523,840	36,887	0	381,422	905,262
78	13.7%	523,840	112,682	467,487	36,789	0	417,144	884,631
79	1.4%	467,487	113,809	358,629	36,555	0	455,876	814,505
80	12.0%	358,629	114,947	272,924	0	0	497,846	770,770

KEY OBSERVATIONS:

The age 80 value in One- Bucket Brian's Account:
$605,070

The age 80 value in Two-Bucket Benjamin's Account: $770,770

Advantage for Two-Bucket Benjamin:
$165,700

As mentioned earlier, Brian and Benjamin both began withdrawals at the same age with the same total assets at age 65. They each withdrew the same amounts each year. **Yet, Benjamin had $165,700 more in his account at age 80, and with less risk. How is this possible?**

Pretty simple. Benjamin heeded his advisor's advice when he recommended putting a portion of his retirement account into an indexed life (or indexed annuity) account. With this strategy, he did not exacerbate his losses by having to withdraw (sell) in a down market. Benjamin could make retirement income withdrawals from his Indexed Universal Life or his Indexed Annuity in the years when the stock market crashed. Remember, you have no stock market losses in an indexed vehicle in the nasty years like 1987, 2000, 2001, 2008 and ???. Brian, on the other hand, did not have that luxury. He had just one bucket and that bucket had a hole in it.

MANAGING YOUR RMD'S

The Two-Bucket strategy is also your hero when it comes to your RMD's.

The Required Minimum Distribution (RMD) rules for qualified plans force retirees who are age 71.5 to take withdrawals from their qualified plans whether they want to or not. If that's you, then during the year of your retirement when you turn 70.5, a withdrawal from your qualified retirement plan based on life expectancy tables is required.

If, for example you are now age 72, the RMD factor based on current Uniform Lifetime Tables is 3.65 percent. So, if the balance in your qualified plan on December 31 of the previous year was $1,500,000, you must take a RMD withdrawal of $54,750. Each year going forward, this RMD percentage increases. At age 80, for example, the required withdrawal, based on current Uniform Lifetime Tables has increased to 5.35 percent of your account balance.

The IRS penalty for not taking this withdrawal is a nasty 50 percent on the shortage. So, if you were age 72 last year, and your IRA RMD amount was $25,000 but you only withdrew $10,000 by year end, the shortage is $15,000. Your penalty tax would be $7,500 (50 percent of $15,000).

Now, let's go back to One-Bucket Brian. He's age 75 with all of his qualified retirement assets in the stock market. His RMD that year is $45,000 and another 2008 happens where the S & P 500 Index lost a whopping 40 percent. Brian is now forced to make his RMD withdrawals when he least wants to . . . in a severely down market.

Two-Bucket Benjamin, on the other hand, sips his Diet Coke by the seashore and makes his RMD withdrawals from his Indexed Annuity knowing that zero is his hero when the stock market crashes.

CONVERGENCE AT THE CORE:

- Be smart and balance your hard-earned retirement account with a Two-Bucket Strategy.
- Creating more options for your retirement withdrawals is a smart move.
- Don't allow the RMD rule to force you to sell in a down market.

WHAT'S NEXT?

In the next chapter, we will show you show you the **difference between nest egg and cash flow.**

PART 3

RESULTS

9

It's About Cash Flow!

"Money is a terrible master but an excellent servant."

P.T. Barnum

Mike and Karen are a sharp couple. They are talented and giving, love people, skilled in their profession, and are making a difference in the lives of others.

When I met them, they were 10 years from retirement and were concerned about having adequate retirement income. All of their retirement assets were in the stock market and their stock market accounts had not done well. Their adviser of many years had never talked to them about the distribution phase of their planning, so they had no clue how much retirement income they could create. What was created, instead, was a lot of concern.

I wish I could tell you that their story is the exception, but it is not. Over and over, people schedule appointments with me, and I quickly discover that they have no idea how much income their current retirement assets will produce.

FOCUS ON CASH FLOW

I did an initial analysis for Mike and Karen and presented them with two options for creating retirement cash flow:

- **Option 1:** Keep doing what you are doing. Keep your retirement money in your stock market account. If your stock market account never has a loss in the future (yeah, right) and your account yields an average of 10 percent per year (8 percent net after fees), you will create initial retirement income in ten years of around **$96,500 per year.** This income amount assumes annual withdrawals of four percent of your account value, which is the retirement income recommendation of most stock market advisers.

- **Option 2:** Reposition your retirement assets into a combination of the financial resources outlined in Section Two of this book. This design will create retirement income of around **$137,000 per year** with **no risk of stock market losses.** Here we assume that the future performance of the financial vehicles selected is equal to the performance over the past 10 years.

Which route do you think they chose?
Which route would you choose?
Exactly.

RETIREMENT CASH FLOW COMPARISON

Plan A: Continue with your brokerage account (Stocks & Mutual Funds)

Plan B: Follow your Financial Convergence Roadmap to creat secured income

RISK OF LOSSES?

YES

NO

$96,000/YR.* initial income amount

$137,000/YR.** initial income amount

*Assumes 8% net return after fees. Withdrawals of 4% of account value per year in retirement.

**Assumes returns based on the past 10-year performance on a specific Fixed Indexed Annuity product.

ACCUMULATION VS. DISTRIBUTION

Your Financial Convergence Roadmap requires coordination of two financial routes.

- Route A is the **Accumulation Phase.**
- Route D is the **Distribution Phase.**

Peter and Josh

Let's say that two guys, we will call them Peter and Josh, both reach the end of Route A with nest eggs of $1,000,000. However, when they merge unto Route D and begin the Distribution Phase, Peter creates $40,000 per year of annual income and Josh creates $90,000 per year. In addition, Peter is losing some of his money to taxes while Josh's $90,000 is 100 percent tax-free.

How is this possible?

Josh's adviser understood the difference between nest egg and cash flow. So, fifteen years ago, he helped Josh design a strategy to maximize his retirement income with no risk of losses. Peter's adviser, on the other hand, focused totally on nest egg planning.

My experience has been that most retirement planners focus on Route A (accumulation) and very little attention given to Route D (distribution). They wrongly assume that if they create the nest egg, the cash flow will take care of itself.

To be sure, you can't create retirement income without creating retirement assets. However, it is critical that if one of your key goals is to maximize lifetime income, then you must focus on the convergent strategies and vehicles which are designed to maximize retirement income.

As the above example demonstrates, it is possible for two individuals to have the same size nest egg, yet their retirement cash flows are dramatically different.

CASH FLOW STRATEGIES WITH STOCK MARKET AND MUTUAL FUND ACCOUNTS:

Many stock market advisers have just one retirement cash flow strategy for their clients: withdraw 3.5 to 4 percent of your nest egg as income each year. If your goal is to maximize your retirement income, there is a better way.

Why don't they encourage their clients to withdraw 7 to 8 percent, instead of 4 percent? Because they know that in the stock market environment, 1987, 2000, 2001, 2002 and 2008 will likely happen again. And when the next crash comes, they don't want egg (not to be confused with nest egg) on their face when they are forced to recommend a reduction in retirement withdrawals so their client does not run out of money.

A few things you should know about the mindset of many stock market advisers when it comes to the Distribution Phase of your planning:

- First, their concern of your running out of retirement money is valid. Everyone knows that the stock market is a roller coaster ride and when you are in the Distribution Phase of your journey, you don't have the luxury of "riding it out" when the next crash hits. Therefore, advisers are forced to be conservative with their withdrawal recommendation.

- Secondly, stock market advisers make their money on fees, whether you have gains in your account or not. Those fees generally range from one to two percent of your account value. If your money is moved out of the stock market environment, recurring fee income to your adviser declines. Nobody likes a pay cut.
- Thirdly, many stock market advisers simply have not explored the value of the secured income strategies outlined in this book. Their world is consumed with trying to figure out the right stock market allocations for their clients.

ROUTE D PLANNING

The conventional wisdom in the stock market planning world is to move your account to more conservative stock market allocations as you approach retirement. The problem with these conservative models is that your potential returns are also reduced, further adding to the cash flow problem with stock market accounts.

In the final chapter, we will bring it all together and show you the numbers. Then you can decide for yourself which cash flow strategy creates the financial convergence that you desire.

The best time to do Route D planning is 10 years or more years before retirement. The second-best time is today! So even if you are near or in retirement, do not despair. We can help you customize a convergence strategy that will give you peace of mind.

CONVERGENCE AT THE CORE:

- There is a big difference between nest egg and cash flow.
- Good retirement planning requires bi-focal vision; one eye on your nest egg and one eye on maximizing future cash flow.
- Is your current plan designed for cash-flow convergence?

WHAT'S NEXT?

The proof is in the puddin'. In the next chapter, we will provide a hands-on **demonstration of creating more income with less risk.**

10

Convergence Delivered

> "The four most expensive words in the English language are, 'This time it's different.'"

Sir John Templeton

The Proof Is in the Puddin'

Ok, let's put our money where our mouth is. Using our **Financial Convergence Roadmap** outlined in Chapter Three, I will demonstrate how we help our clients create more income with less risk.

I will then compare our model with a model where you hold 100 percent of your retirement assets in a stock market or mutual fund account. I will even assume favorable returns on your stock market funds, such as a 9-to-10 percent return (8 percent net of fees) with no losses over the next 40 years. (Remember, the S & P 500 Index did around four percent over the first 15 years of this century.)

I DESIGN, YOU DECIDE

Meet John and Lisa. John is age 57 and Lisa is 56. They have four adult children. Both John and Lisa have good jobs, enjoy the outdoors, and plan to retire in about 10 years. John contributes to a 401(k) program at work, which has an employer match of three percent. Both John and Lisa have rollover IRA accounts. They have an additional $30,000 per year available to go toward creating additional retirement income. Currently, all of their retirement funds are in the stock market.

FINANCIAL ASSETS SUMMARY:

- Traditional IRA $625,000
- 401(k) Account $125,000

- Roth IRA $200,000
- Mutual Fund Account $100,000
- Annual Contributions $30,000/year
- Social Security @ age 67 $25,000/year

Financial Convergence – Step 1

The first thing we did was have a convergence conversation to help John and Lisa identify their key financial values. Here's a summary:

- "Protecting our principal from losses is important to us."
- "More modest, secure, and steady returns of five-to-seven percent fit our values more than the potential of higher returns, which have the risk of crashes like 1987, 2001 and 2008."
- "We want the focus to be on maximizing our retirement cash flow, not on how big our nest egg is. We want strategies and vehicles that are designed to maximize our retirement income."

- "We would like more retirement income during the first five years of retirement to provide for more travel."
- "As much as possible, we want to pay tax on the 'seed' not on the 'crop,' as we are concerned that tax rates could increase significantly in the future."
- John said, "I want Lisa to be able to maintain the same standard of living we currently enjoy in the event of my premature death, so adequate life insurance coverage is important."
- "Our focus is not on a large financial inheritance for our heirs. If there is something there, fine. We have helped them with their education and have taught them the importance of personal responsibility and how to create their own opportunities."
- "Simplicity. We do not want to spend time managing our retirement assets. We want strategies that can perform well on auto-pilot."

Financial Convergence – Step 2

Next, we discussed financial goals and time frames.

- John to retire at age 67 with a minimum lifetime income of $150,000 per year and growing.
- Debt free at retirement age.
- Two trips per year to foreign countries during the early years of retirement.
- More income during early years of retirement for travel expenses.

Financial Convergence – Step 3

Based on the goals and values identified by John and Lisa, we are now ready to guide them to the best convergent financial strategies.

CONVERGENT FINANCIAL STRATEGIES:

- Use financial vehicles that create guaranteed lifetime income and protection of principal from stock market crashes.

- Create adequate income replacement in the event of John's death.
- Use strategies that will create tax-free retirement income as much as possible.
- Contribute to John's 401(k) plans during the accumulation phase up to the company match. Move contributions above the match to financial vehicles that better accomplish convergence.
- Move the 401(k) to an IRA at retirement and reposition these assets into indexed vehicles.

Financial Convergence – Step 4

Finally, by knowing John and Lisa's values, goals and strategies, we can help them select the financial vehicles that create financial convergence.

CONVERGENT FINANCIAL VEHICLES:

- Customized High Cash Value Indexed Universal Life
    - No risk of losses on the cash value crediting

- o Historical returns of seven percent or more using selected indexes
- o Tax-free retirement income through properly designed policy loans
- o Tax-free face amount paid to heir in the event of death
- o Designed to maximize retirement cash flow
- Fixed Index Annuity
  - o No risk of losses
  - o Creates guaranteed and increasing lifetime income
  - o Historical returns in the range identified by John and Lisa as acceptable

FINANCIAL VEHICLES WHICH DO NOT CONVERGE FOR JOHN AND LISA AND WHY:

- Stocks and mutual funds
  Risk of losses
  No lifetime income guarantees
  More management required
- Bonds
  - o Low returns
  - o Some risk

- Precious metals
  - Volatility
  - Not income-producing
- Bank savings account
  - Low returns
  - Taxable interest
- Investment real estate
  - Management responsibility
  - Market risk

CONVERGENCE DELIVERED

KEY FEATURES OF THE FINANCIAL CONVERGENCE MODEL FOR JOHN AND LISA:

- Safety of Principal
- Adequate liquidity
- Guaranteed lifetime Income
- Increasing retirement income

ASSUMPTIONS:

- $18,000 annual contributions to 401(k) plan
- Stock market accounts grow at 10 percent (8 percent net after fees) with no losses.

- $30,000 per year new contributions in addition to 401(k)
- IUL returns are projected at 10-year historical returns with a selected carrier and index
- Fixed Index Annuity returns are projected at 10-year historical rates with a selected carrier, product and index

ASSUMED ALLOCATIONS:

- $30,000 per year to the Indexed Universal Life Policy
- Roth Funds to the Indexed Universal Life Policy
- $725,000 (IRA and MF account) to an Fixed Index Annuity
- $125,000 remains in 401(k) account until retirement, then withdrawn as income from ages 67 to 71

LIFETIME INCOME PROJECTIONS:

- **AGE 67-72**
    - $401(k) W/D over 5 years $132,898
    - Fixed Index Annuity $69,228
    - Social Security $25,000
    - **TOTALS:**   **$227,126/year**
- **AGE 72 –77:**
    - Fixed Index Annuity $91,501
    - IUL $83,153
    - Social Security $25,000
    - **TOTALS:**   **$199,654/year**

- **AGE 77-100:**
    - Fixed Index Annuity $110,171
    - IUL $83,153
    - Social Security $25,000
    - **TOTALS:**   **$218,324/year**

ASSUMPTIONS ON ABOVE:

- 10-year historical indexing returns on IUL and Indexed Annuity with a specific carrier
- 401(k) yields a net of five percent per year during withdrawals

CASH FLOW COMPARISON
Risk vs. Secured

Assumptions:

- Stock Market Account: 10 percent (eight percent net return after fees).
- No losses for the next 40 years. Income withdrawals of 4 percent of account value per year.
- Convergence Model: IUL and Annuity returns based on past 10-year performance with a specific carrier and products.

• AGE 67-72	RISK	SECURED
○ Social Security	$25,000	$25,000
○ Retirement assets	$118,489	$211,257
○ **TOTAL INCOME:**	**$143,489**	**$227,126**

- **AGE 72 –77:**
    - Social Security $25,000 $25,000
    - Retirement assets $133,760 $200,416
    - **TOTAL INCOME:**   **$158,760**   **$199,654**

- **AGE 77-100:**
    - Social Security $25,000 $25,000
    - Retirement assets $152,340 $219,517
    - **TOTAL INCOME:**   **$177,340**   **$218,324**

RISK COMPARISON

Our convergence model eliminates the risk of stock market losses. The stock market model does not.

INCOME COMPARISON

**Our Convergence Model creates over a million dollars more income
from age 67 to 85!**

And, remember, we assumed the stock market account would grow at a net return, after fees, of 8 percent with no losses.

Note: To be fair with the stock market account, in the later years, there would be more money to pass on to heirs using the given assumptions. So, if financial legacy was a key value, we would adjust the strategies and vehicles to create the desired balance between income and legacy.

CONVERGENCE AT THE CORE:

- Proper retirement planning requires that you clearly identify your financial values and goals.
- In this chapter, we have demonstrated that It is possible to create more income with less risk.
- Conclusion: Financial Convergence works.

WHAT'S NEXT?

In the final chapter, Enjoying the Journey, we will share ideas on **making your life more enjoyable and purposeful.**

11
Enjoying the Journey

"Happiness is not in the mere
possession of money; it lies in the joy
of achievement, in the thrill of
creative effort."

Franklin D. Roosevelt

A Lesson from the Bighorns

My son, Matt, and I drove 900 miles with 11 other
men, strapped on our 40-pound backpacks, and

began our contest with gravity and minimal oxygen. When we reached the plateau a day later, we set up camp and enjoyed the beautiful trout lakes and fresh streams of the Bighorn Mountains in northeastern Wyoming. I remember my friend, Edgar, saying, "If the water is flowing fast enough to create foam, it is safe to drink."

Life is a journey, and enjoyment comes from more than money (although money helps). We all need a continual flow of the refreshing water of ideas, challenges, and opportunities to keep us on the cutting edge of life, enjoying the journey and avoiding the dangers of a stagnant life.

I like to observe and converse with retired people. Some appear to have pretty much checked out on life, going along from day to day with little purpose, like a meandering river. Others see this phase of their lives as the most exciting of all: a time to experience convergence in powerful ways. These individuals are purposefully engaging their passions, unique abilities, relationships, financial resources, time, and energy to make a lasting difference in their world.

Take, for example, my long-time friend, Paul Kienel. He is now in his eighties and still fully engaged in life. He continues his passions to make a difference in the world of education. A few months ago, I sat down with him for an hour and asked him pointed questions about his life. If was fascinating to hear him share his story. When our hour was over, I walked away thinking to myself, "Wow, Paul's life is truly one of convergence."

He grew up in a single-parent home. His mother did not have much money, but she was determined to provide him with those intangible things which have much greater value than money. She connected him with community leaders who modeled lives of excellence, greatly impacting his world view. During his teenage years, she introduced him to a man who mentored him in the trade of woodworking, a skill that provided the funds he needed to pay his way through college and a source of great enjoyment even to this day.

Throughout his adult life, Paul's passions and skills lifted him to key places of leadership in the field of education. During my conversation with him, it became clear how his life resources – training, skills, education, unique abilities, relationships, habits, time, money, past experiences – all converged into his Big River - excellence in education.

Just recently, Paul and his wife, Annie, received the honor of having a prestigious leadership training center at a California college named after them.

Unfortunately, I have known others who have one goal in life – retirement. They reach that goal and live out the rest of their years with purposeless boredom. Oh yes, they play golf, they take trips, they indulge themselves to the level their financial resources allow. Nothing wrong with golf and trips, but if those things are the goal, life becomes shallow very quickly.

We are never too old to learn and grow. Extraordinary lives are never happenstance. They are the result of the choices we make and the actions we take.

So, I encourage you to build the following habits into your life.

1. **Take a break.** Schedule time away from your daily routine. Do it quarterly. Make it a

priority. This is your time for thinking, reflecting, reading, and creating. Get alone. Get quiet. Leave your cell phone at home. Find a restful place. Start thinking outside the box. Think about Yitron: The Hebrew word that describes those deposits into the lives of others that live on long after you are gone. Think about your passions. Think about something big, something meaningful. Take lots of notes. Draw diagrams. Create a game plan. Get after it.   The sparkling waters of fresh ideas will make you smile a lot! You should have lots of unfinished projects when you die.

Remember:

Work is expending effort on things we don't want to do;

Passion is expending energy on things we love to do.

The goal is to do no work!

2. Use your head.

Every new idea has three phases. Phase one is the **Creation** of the idea. When a new idea is birthed, excitement flows and possibilities and opportunities begin to emerge in your mind. You can't write them down fast enough. This is the fun part.

Phase two is not so fun, but be ready for it because it will come. Phase two is the **Challenges** phase. Here the development of your idea begins to encounter obstacles and setbacks. When this happens, and it surely will, the temptation will be to become discouraged and abandon your idea. The temptation will be to shift your focus away from the idea and on to the rapids and dams that try to drown out the vitality and viability of your idea. You are now at a critical point. If not handled correctly, you will swim to shore and your idea will settle at the bottom of the river and die.

However, your mind has an amazing capacity to take the challenges and turn them on their heads. You must first know that your mind has this ability and you must persevere until the breakthrough comes. I call this phase **Conversion,** where you train your mind to convert the challenges into even greater opportunities. This is the mind ability used by Thomas Edison, George Washington Carver, General Patton, Steve Jobs, Henry Ford, Colonel Sanders and many others. These people understood that obstacles and challenges can become either a stumbling block or a stepping stone. When challenges are correctly viewed as catalysts to stretch your thinking and imagination and deepen your resolve with a never-give-up attitude, you will not necessarily enjoy them, but you will later look back and see how important they were for your greater success.

USE YOUR HEAD

3. **Shift Your Paradigm.** Expand your creativity by studying outside the familiar. Several years ago, Joel Barker from Eden Prairie, Minnesota produced some powerful videos on paradigm shifts. His research clearly demonstrated that the most significant breakthroughs in any field came most often from people on the outside. Why? Because their minds had not been taken captive by the enemy of familiarity. For decades, the Swiss were the world leaders in making watches. But when the digital watch concept was presented to them, they rejected it. They couldn't see beyond tiny moving parts.

Today, the digital watch you are wearing was most likely made in Japan.

4. **Build Life Convergence.** Convergence works in all areas of life, not just finances. So, build a life convergence model for yourself using the diagram below. For every decision you make, every project you launch, every new endeavor you undertake, build a convergence model and watch your thinking, planning and results explode to new levels.

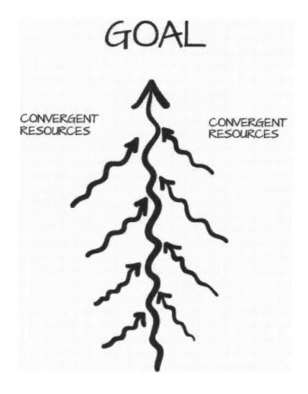

CONVEGENCE AT THE CORE:

- Life is a journey. Make it an enjoyable one.
- Shake things up by getting away from the routine and think deeply on stuff that matters a lot.
- Use your head. Remember the Creation-Challenges-Conversion process.
- Begin and end every day thinking about growing a life of convergence.

WHAT'S NEXT?

Read the book again: underline, take notes (use the notes section provided), strategize, think, plan, discuss with your spouse and trusted friends. Work on your Financial Convergence Roadmap. As you do, I believe you will discover that:

Creating more income with less risk is the smart thing to do!

Questions? Let's talk.

Contact me at: Dave@compassgrouponline.com

Or

www.compassgrouponline.com

**PRINTABLE
CONVERGENCE PLANNING TOOLS
@**

WWW.COMPASSGROUPONLINE.COM

ENDNOTES

1. Tom Rath, *Strengths Finder 2.0*
2. Robert Clinton, *The Making of a Leader*
3. Jim Collins, *Built to Last*
4. *http://www.multpl.com/s-p-500-historical-prices/table/by-year*
5. Source: http://www.cnn.com/2009/POLITICS/04/15/walker.tax.debt/
6. *https://www.law.cornell.edu/uscode/text/26/7702*
7. Ed Slott, *The Retirement Savings Time Bomb and How to Diffuse It*
8. Nelson Nash, *Infinite Banking*
9. http://blogs.wsj.com/moneybeat/2014/05/09/just-how-dumb-are-investors?
10. https://dqydj.com/sp-500-return-calculator/
11. *http://www.barrons.com/articles/retirement-rules-time-to-rethink-a-4-withdrawal-rate-1428722900*

Acknowledgements

I began thinking about a book on convergence several years ago. Having observed the countless hours that my wife, Lynda, a gifted author, devoted to the writing of her many books, I knew that this was not a casual undertaking. It would require personal commitment along with the talents of a strong support team to make it happen. Thankfully, I was provided such a team.

Lynda was my "in-house" resource, to whom I would go often to tap into her experience and wisdom.

My personal assistant, Jessica Hulstrom, was given the task of formatting and organizing the book, and she did a masterful job.

Corrin Brewer, a rising star as an illustrator, provided her ideas and skills in producing the hand-drawn illustrations as well as the book cover.

Stan Nelson, a seasoned veteran in design, also provided valuable diagrams and illustrations.

Thanks also goes to my close friend and talented entrepreneur, Thor Iverson, who offered encouragement, ideas and valuable feedback over the many months on this project.

Finally, I owe a great debt of gratitude to my many clients who have placed their trust in me and who, over the years, have helped to shape the contents of this book.

About the Author

David A. Bjorklund, CLU, ChFC, founder and president of the Compass Group, is a well-known financial educator in Monument, Colorado. He has been a financial consultant for more than 30 years and has conducted financial and leadership seminars across the United States.

Dave's professional mission is to help his clients and their families achieve convergence in all areas of their lives and make a permanent mark on their world. As a financial consultant, his focus is on helping his clients achieve financial freedom by growing their wealth safely and securely.

Dave and his wife, Lynda, have six children and twelve grandchildren. When he is not working with his clients or spending time with family, he loves to play basketball or hike the mountains of Colorado.

Dave has served in leadership roles with several local and national charities.

Personal Planning Notes

Made in the
USA
Lexington, KY